THERE IS ALWAYS HOPE

Overcoming Life's Challenges Successfully

SHEILA M. DORSEY

Published by S. Marie Books

CONTENTS

There Is Always Hope:

Overcoming Life's Challenges Successfully

ISBN-13: 978-0-578-69657-7

Published by *S. Marie Books*

Printed in the United States of America.

This book is available at special quantity discounts for bulk purchases, for sales promotions, fund-raising, and educational needs. For information, please write smarie13d@yahoo.com.

DEDICATION

*I dedicate this book to my family and friends who kept me in their prayers daily and offered support during some difficult moments in my life.
I also like to dedicate this book to individuals who need encouragement and hope.*

ACKNOWLEDGMENTS

I will always be so grateful, appreciative, and thankful to God for keeping me focused and placing me on a spiritual path in making this accomplishment possible for me. Writing a book for the first time was not easy; it was hard and scary, but with a great publisher, we made *There Is Always Hope* happen.

I thank my mom, Beverly A. Dorsey, whom I love dearly, for listening to my ideas on many occasions and for believing that I could do this.

Thank you, Chantel Ford, for believing in me and connecting me with my publisher, Wanza Leftwich. Thank you, Wanza Leftwich, for helping me bring this book to life.

I appreciate and love my family and friends who had faith in me and believed that I could achieve my goal of writing a book. As my grandmother use to say, "You never know what you can do if you don't try."

INTRODUCTION

For many years now, I have wanted to write a book, but I procrastinated year after year. Has that been your experience with something you've always wanted to do? You want to, but you don't have enough motivation to actually do it? Why is it that we have goals and God-given talents, but we delay in achieving those goals or putting our talents to use? Well, one day, I just decided it was time to put myself first. With so much going on in the world that we have to endure, I felt it was time for me to achieve my goal of writing a book and, at the same time, help someone else achieve theirs. I decided to write about issues related to people's feelings and the difficulties they have with adjusting after some type of devastating event happens. I want to make a difference in the lives of people who think there is no solution to their problem.

Because of my passion for people, I decided to write a book on topics that might help you better understand how you can move forward after losing a loved one, getting a divorce, losing a job, or any other difficult life event. I hope that this book will give each of us a better understanding of how to manage life's challenges.

Many of us experience depression that brings with it sadness and a lack of focus and energy. It may be due to a loss or a chemical imbalance, but most don't know how to manage the symptoms, where to go for assistance, or what to do when that moment of depression comes. I, too, have experienced depression, much sadness, and heartbreak in my life, but I thank God for leading me to a better path mentally and physically regardless of what challenges I faced. I pray you will begin to walk this path with me.

PART 1

1

LIFE'S CHALLENGES

As a teenager, I grew up in a home with an individual who suffered from a chronic disease—alcoholism. Because of this, my family and I experienced a lot of mental and emotional turmoil. I would personally try to avoid going home because I did not want to experience another day or night of household confusion. Many nights I could not sleep or concentrate on my studies or enjoy my life. Although there were many resources along with treatments available during this time, for whatever reason, this individual did not seek help. Alcoholism is a disease that is difficult to overcome, and it causes much pain for the individual and everyone around them. Alcoholics tend to mask their feelings to the point where most of us would probably say they have everything under control, but they usually don't. I could not understand how someone could have such a disease and not want to seek help.

Many of us are looking for an escape route or trying to find help, but we are not sure where to go to find it. We are faced with so many obstacles that, at times, we feel overwhelmed. We often think that no one cares, but in reality, many do. Sometimes people are just not sure how to show they care. Knowing how much we all need loving care and attention from those around us, we should make every effort to show we care by motivating and encouraging those in our circle of associates, friends, and family members, letting them know we are there to help. No one can fix a broken situation, but we should be able to encourage those whose spirits need to be lifted. No one should ever feel they are alone.

When I experience physical, mental, and emotional challenges, I look for ways to work through them or try and find solutions by using methods such as reading, walking, meditating, practicing yoga, and listening to soft music. If that doesn't work, it's okay to seek help from a professional counselor, your pastor, or someone you feel you can trust. I sometimes have difficulty sharing with others what I go through, but what I have learned is that sometimes I need to just let it all out. I feel relieved and much healthier after doing so.

I have listed below some of the methods I've used to cope with my personal challenges. I pray they will be a source of strength and encouragement for you:

Meditation

Sometimes we need to find a quiet space where we can just think and reevaluate our daily experiences, good or bad. This allows us to better focus on the most important issues of the day. When we stay focused, it helps us keep our minds on things that are peaceful and positive. This also allows us to spend our one-on-one time alone with God and to meditate on His Word.

Yoga

Yoga is another method that can be used to relax and de-stress. This discipline is used by many for various reasons. I find that when I'm feeling stressed or simply losing focus, yoga helps my mind and body relax. I also listen to different types of music, the ones that help me find the peace I need.

In this beautiful world we live in, there are and will be many challenges that we will be faced with, and unfortunately, no one will be exempt from this. I have faced challenges in my relationships, finances, career, etc. and I used to think I was being punished for something I did or did not do in God's eyes. Even though I feel that I treat people with respect and show them compassion, and I'm usually there for them when they need me, for some reason, I lost friendships and didn't know why. I struggled to understand the reason the relationships failed and tried to work through my issues. I called this "self-pity." One thing I am sure of is that not releasing or talking about something that's heavy on your mind and heart can cause mental and physical health issues. At one point, I felt too embarrassed to speak with anyone, including family and friends. I didn't want anyone to judge me or repeat how I was feeling to someone else. I truly believe in confidentiality, but not everyone does.

There were many times I've cried, did not sleep well, and worried about my difficult circumstances and those of others. This has made me very confused because I could not figure out how to work through my issues. Then I had to stop and realize I wasn't being punished; God was trying to get me to be still so that I could see His favor in each storm. Going through storms may not feel so good at first, but you eventually become aware that the dark clouds are rolling away, and it's going to be okay. Storms help us become stronger and prepare us for the next one that comes our way and the next one after that.

In the past several years, many of my loved ones and friends who were very dear to me have passed away. Some had long-term illnesses, and others were sudden deaths. Sudden deaths have been the worst to deal with in my experience, but any death of a loved one or friend causes so much heartbreak and pain. I was not sure of how to handle that pain, but I knew my dear ones would have wanted me to move on and enjoy a healthy life. How do we continue through life without that person? A very wise person once told me that it's okay to grieve, and it's good to do so, but it's also important to continue our lives. Moving on with our lives helps us stay focused on a healthy life. Our loved ones will never be forgotten; we carry them with us in our hearts.

In order to continue living a healthy life, I had to learn of the many resources that were available to help me through each new challenge. It's funny how as children, we never think about death, being stressed, or worried about anything, but as adults, things are very different, and we sometimes encounter health challenges that require quick decisions. When experiencing depression and sadness, our minds carry so many burdens that we oftentimes cannot handle. Our brains become so overloaded with worry and pain that they cause us to shut down both mentally and physically. Because of this, precious time in our lives passes us by, and we don't always know how to get back on track and move forward.

I have also experienced having individuals lash out at me for reasons that I could not understand. I truly believe they were experiencing something in their own lives that they neglected to completely work through. Sometimes we just don't understand what causes people to act out. It's important to learn how to cope with life's many challenges so we can enjoy all that God has blessed us with in spite of what we are going through. Life is filled with beauty and lots of love, and we should focus on that instead of the pain.

I have faced many days where I kept so much bottled up inside. I wanted to talk to someone but was not sure if others would understand or if they would judge me. Sad to say, but some of us don't know when to keep things private and when it's time to open up. People often share their life stories with me. I listen and what they tell me I keep confidential. I do, at times, share my thoughts with them about their situation, encourage them, and sometimes offer advice. Many people who know me would probably say I offer advice a lot. What I'm doing must work for them because they come back again for more. If I offer my advice, it's because I have experienced the same or something very similar. I'm glad to be there for others and encourage them when needed. Everyone needs a friend.

REFLECTION

Journal Questions

1. What would you do if you were faced with an alcoholic in
   your family? How would you help this person?
2. Would you seek help, or would you ignore the problem?
3. How would you handle the passing of a loved one or
   special friend?

PART 2

2
LIFE

Life is beautiful. Each day brings us peace, happiness, sadness, and disappointments, and each situation helps us grow as we learn from the many successes and failures we are faced with. Life allows each of us to select our own goals and make our own decisions.

We all handle life changes and challenges very differently, but I want you to understand that there is a light at the end of the tunnel. We face many unexpected changes that revolve around losing a loved one, getting a divorce, losing a job, becoming homeless, enduring broken relationships, etc.

I truly believe that if we put God first and include Him in our daily decisions, everything will eventually fall into place. There's nothing too big or too difficult for our God to handle. We may not always fully understand why certain things happen or don't happen to us, but please know that with God, we can take on anything we are faced with and win.

God provides each of us with specific talents to use for His glory, but many of us procrastinate on using those talents or gifts. Sometimes, we put off our dreams for using our talents until later in life in order to support others. That would be me.

We are taught that once we accept Jesus into our lives, establish a relationship with Him, worship Him and study His word, we will be able to better understand how to handle most of the difficult situations in our lives. We may not always understand Him, but when we continue to pray and ask God for guidance and understanding, He gives them to each of us in His own timing and not ours. I love God so much.

Sometimes I wish I had what it takes to save the entire world and all the people in it, but realistically I know that this is not possible. Over the years, friends, co-workers, neighbors, and family members, etc., have shared with me some difficult situations they have experienced or were recently faced with. I listened to what they were going through, and sometimes I would give my personal opinion in the hopes that I could encourage them to be strong and hold on. I reminded them that God is only a step away.

When they tell me of a situation that I have also gone through or if I am very familiar with what they are now going through, I share my opinion or something I did that has worked for me. It is important that I show compassion, be a good listener, and let people know how caring I am. I also provide them with resources that might assist them or if they just want to talk, I make myself available.

God gives us all purpose and many special spiritual gifts that we don't always understand. There was a time when I did not understand my purpose in life or the many gifts that I demonstrated. Through prayer, God gave me a better understanding of my purpose and gifts. We often don't realize the number of spiritual gifts we've been blessed with. Our spiritual gifts can be in the form of love, showing support to someone who is going through a difficult situation, encouragement, financial giving, etc. When we show love and compassion from the heart to someone, it does something to our souls. I love it when God places me exactly where I need to be.

When someone shares their dreams and goals with you, show your support to them by encouraging them in their endeavors. This is a blessing to them and you as well. I think we sometimes forget that God offers gifts not only to *some* of us but *all* of us. Don't ever worry that someone will get more than you. Encourage each other, and your seasons of blessings will come in due time. When someone is feeling down and out, it is the responsibility of a Christian or a kindhearted person to let them know that their situation is only temporary. Pray with them and for them and keep them encouraged.

Let's focus on giving. If we can help someone who may need money, clothing, food, or a ride to a store, we should help that person. You never know; it may be *you* someday. Sometimes we tend to help the same people over and over, but it's okay to help others as well. Hard times and hardships have no date and timestamp.

I remember experiencing some difficult times while raising my daughter as a single parent. Having my daughter was a blessing, but it was also demanding, and sometimes there were quick decisions I had to make alone. I was very much afraid during my pregnancy, and sometimes I felt alone and was not sure if I could successfully raise a child alone. During that time, I will never forget my constant prayers and my many one-on-one times with God. By having a relationship with God and offering up so many prayers, I was able to focus on the gift that I was about to receive and not focus on whether I could handle being a single parent. You see, sometimes we focus on the what if's and not our blessing.

I do realize that there will be times when what I've planned may not happen the way I want it to, but I do know that God is alive. He's waiting for us to reach out to Him, and that is what I did. Looking back, I smile and sometimes cry, but I will always thank God for blessing me with the courage to raise a respectful and wonderful daughter. I will admit, being a single parent means hard work, prioritizing, constantly providing, but most importantly, loving and caring for my daughter. I had to be sure I was raising my daughter in a decent neighborhood, in good schools, and that I had funds for after-school activities. I had to be sure the bills were paid and figure out my next steps. I faced many financial hardships and other struggles, but I refused to let any of them bring me down. I also struggled with pride by not asking for help, but sometimes we must put our pride aside and reach out to others for help. This was very hard for me but, knowing the type of family I had and still have, asking for help when needed was no problem. My family stepped in many times to assist me and my daughter. I will never forget how blessed I was to have such a wonderful family.

When looking back on my past struggles and challenges, I realize how much each situation has helped me to grow, learn, and be grateful and appreciative. I am not saying that I will have no more struggles and challenges, but my past has helped me to become a stronger individual. From my past to today, I have been so blessed to have accomplished many wonderful things in life, such as raising a beautiful daughter, having a home, a good job, and good health. We should never allow our past struggles to overshadow the wonderful and great blessing that God has for our future.

REFLECTION

Journal Questions

1. Do you include God in your daily decisions? If so, how?
2. Do you procrastinate on your accomplishments for others?
3. How do you handle difficult situations?
4. Do you understand your purpose in life?

PART 3

DEPRESSION AND SADNESS

Depression and sadness can cause your body to mentally and physically shut down. They cause our personalities to change and sometimes make us withdraw from our families, friends, and others. However, people don't always understand what you are going through. When you are experiencing this, others may not understand or might think you are angry with them or dislike them for some reason, but you should let them know it is not true. I have experienced many challenges in my life that have caused me to become sad and sometimes depressed like others. Feeling this way will cause us to withdraw from others and want to be alone, but we can figure out how to handle what we are going through. I think it's important to talk about the reasons why we want to withdraw, but that's up to each individual. No one should ever force the issue or put pressure on another person.

Depression and sadness can sometimes cause us to become bitter, but if we don't admit our problems, it can become very difficult for people to want to be around us. When we don't try to work through this, we are only allowing the devil to steal our joy and each beautiful day that God has blessed us with. It's hard speaking to someone about your experiences and finding someone you trust enough to talk to about your concerns. Try to work through these challenges by focusing on more positive things or take in a movie, treat yourself to dinner, as I sometimes do.

I used to ask, "Where is the light at the end of the tunnel that we all hear about?" When we are down and out, the best thing we can do for ourselves is have a private conversation with our Lord and Savior. When we are still and quiet, God speaks to us in ways we will probably never understand. We need to understand that God is closer to us than we think (myself included). God listens, teaches us, comforts us, and, most importantly, in due time, He will answer our prayers as He sees fit. He understands what we are going through, but we must have patience and give Him time to work it out. For our good. Why do we trust man so much but not our God?

I know that it's not easy to go through heartbreak and pain, but this is real, and we must find ways to go through and manage our depression and sadness. Why is it that we can trust man to work out our situations by supplying us with drugs and alcohol, but we don't give God a chance to work with us on our many challenges and daily problems? I have heard many pastors say, "Your outlook determines your outcome." Do you think this is true? Of course, you do! That statement is true and correct. You would be amazed at what God can do for you through prayer, believing, and trusting Him. Give God a chance. He will show you how to work through any situation you are faced with in life. He is the greatest friend you will ever have.

I'm sitting here this afternoon thinking about both my past and current challenges. Some bring tears, and some make me smile. However, I know that no matter what I go through, God is near and will always watch and protect not only me but you too. There will be many times when we are feeling our lowest and won't understand why we are facing bad experiences or challenges in our lives. We need to understand that there is a GOD who is fair, forgiving, and non-judgmental and always near when we need Him.

REFLECTION

Journal Questions

1. Do you believe in God? If so, why?
2. How do you overcome depression and sadness?
3. If you are struggling to overcome depression, will you
   seek professional help?

PART 4

4

RELATIONSHIPS AND BREAK-UPS

We often become very depressed, sad, and sometimes experience a physical shutdown due to failed relationships and break-ups. This is not always easy, especially when there is no closure to your story. Love can sometimes be a little tricky. When you love someone or have that special closeness, break-ups are never easy, and they can sometimes be devastating and may take some time to overcome. I've been in relationships I thought were great, but later realized how completely wrong this person was for me. I have been mentally abused by what someone said to me, which caused me to physically shut down.

No one should be disrespected in a relationship. Relationships should be an enjoyable, learning experience with lots of demonstrated love. I didn't understand how someone could be so disrespectful, nasty, and mean and think of it as love. I'm not ashamed to talk about my experiences and how I had to learn to take control of my own happiness. We should never allow anyone to make us feel like we are not good enough for them or that we are not worthy of being with them. Maybe they are not worthy of you. At the beginning of many relationships, both people seem to communicate using the same language, wanting to achieve the same goals and wanting to grow into the relationship together, but later, you learn that they no longer want to be in the relationship. This sometimes causes depression and sadness.

I'm not sure if we will ever understand why it's so difficult to tell someone the truth, that you no longer want to be in a relationship. It's just that easy. I do understand that sometimes God will send us seasonal people as a test but will later come back and remove what I would call *toxic people* from our lives with good reason. And yes, we should be thankful. We should never settle for anyone who is not the right one for us.

There are so many people who are broken or have unresolved issues that they take to new relationships without discussing what caused the break-up in the first place. We must understand that every person and every relationship is different. In maintaining a healthy relationship, we should never apply our past relationship mistakes to our present relationships. We should never allow a person to take away our joy and happiness. Our joy belongs to each of us.

Many, many people are so broken, but whose responsibility is it to fix them? *Not yours.* What we can do is encourage and pray for them, but we cannot fix or change anyone. We all know someone who may be experiencing difficult situations in areas like these—I'll include myself—but we don't always talk about them. In my case, due to trust issues, I kept a lot inside. My grandmother used to tell me it's okay to talk with your family and friends, but her advice was to take all of my concerns and problems to *God* in silent prayer. She said He would work them out in His time and not mine. So often we think that we have everything under control, but we usually don't. I became so stressed because I kept so much inside, and I bet you have too. You really need to release your problems to a special friend, pastor, or someone you feel you can trust, but my first choice will always be to give them to God.

If we don't release our stress over life's difficulties to God, we can easily become bitter, unhappy, lash out at others, can't sleep, and may develop health problems that could cause us to unnecessarily pop pills, drink alcohol and even do drugs. Why is it that we think we can handle all of our problems alone? The truth is that we are human and not as strong as we think we are. We should never be discouraged to the point where we don't seek anyone's help or advice, if necessary, to overcome challenges that we are faced with. We must always remember the most important thing: forgiveness. When we forgive someone and pray for them, it brings peace to our hearts and souls.

There are a variety of resources available from many different spiritual leaders that are helpful or that might assist each of us in different ways. Check your church's bookstore, get recommendations from your pastor or fellow church members or from online Christian resources. I am praying for you, and please remember: There is always hope.

REFLECTION

Journal Questions

1. Have you ever experienced a bad break-up? How did you feel afterward?
2. Is there an easy way to tell someone that you want out of a relationship? Shouldn't you be honest with this person?
3. Have you ever been in a relationship where the other person displayed bad behavior that was caused by unresolved issues in their past?

PART 5

5

DISAPPOINTMENTS

As we know, we will all have to experience some form of disappointment in our lives. We must learn to accept and release those disappointments. I have personally experienced many back-to-back disappointments and wondered if I would ever get through them. Once we find ways to release our disappointment, it will help us move on to a healthy life. Disappointments can be very painful, emotional, and sometimes frustrating. Disappointments can also help each of us to become stronger and develop a deeper relationship with God. We will experience many forms of disappointments, such as not getting the job, the home or vehicle we applied for, failed marriages and relationships, disappointments with our children, etc.

We have had people come in and out of our lives, some who just walked away with no explanation or closure. But I have learned to accept and focus on how to work through these disappointments in a more positive and spiritual way. I'm learning every day how to choose to be in the presence of encouraging and motivating people. The truth is, we all need each other. I also realize that everyone you share your stories of disappointment with may not understand or be there for you. What I do know is we all have a story. Sometimes we just need to stay focused on our goals, motivated, encourage ourselves, and be careful not to always put others before ourselves.

REFLECTION

Journal Questions

1. Sometimes disappointments can be stressful and emotional. How easy is it for you to accept disappointments?
2. Do you feel mentally stronger after overcoming your disappointments?
3. Do you allow past situations to disappoint you?

REFERENCES & RESOURCES

1. Jeremiah 32:17
2. Philippians 4:6-7
3. Romans 8:28
4. Hebrews 11:1
5. Your pastors and ministers
6. Christian counseling
7. Professional counseling